# Spring Harvest Bible Workbook

GW00382206

## First-century Game Changers: Studies From Acts

**6 sessions for small groups**

Mission

elevation ⬢    Spring Harvest

written in partnership with

HOPE
in our villages, towns & cities

First published in 2016 by Elevation for Spring Harvest

Elevation is part of Memralife Group, registered charity number 1126997, a company limited by guarantee, registered in England and Wales, number 6667924. 14 Horsted Square, Uckfield, East Sussex, TN22 1QG

British Library Cataloguing in Publication Data

A catalogue record for this book is available from the British Library

ISBN 978-1-911237-03-7

Designed by Ascent Creative
Printed by Halcyon

**Thank you to Steve Clifford, Dr Rachel Jordan and Rev Yemi Adedeji who commissioned the Talking Jesus report on behalf of the Evangelical Alliance, the Church of England, the One People Commission and HOPE. Thanks too to Catherine Butcher for her work developing this study guide.**

# Contents

# About this book

This book is written primarily for groups to use - both established groups meeting regularly for Bible study and prayer, and groups formed specifically to explore mission in their local church context. It can also be used by individuals who want to explore mission in Acts and its application today. The group might be drawn from one church or several churches in an area. You might use the term home groups, Bible study groups, cell groups – we've used the term 'group' as the generic term.

Our hope and prayer is that these six studies will be part of a journey with lasting implications for the group, the churches represented by those involved, and the communities and networks where God has placed you. We want this to be more than six Bible studies. Each study includes practical application to enable you to be game-changers in your family, work-place and community.

It is perhaps helpful to spell out the assumptions that we have made about the groups that will use these studies.

- The emphasis on the studies will be on the application of the Bible. Group members will not just learn facts, but will be encouraged to think, 'How does this apply to me?' What change does this require of me? In what incidents and situations in my life is this relevant?'

- Groups can encourage honesty and make space for questions and doubts. The aim of the studies is not to find the 'right answer', but to help members understand the Bible by working through their questions. The Christian faith throws up paradoxes. Events in people's lives may make particular verses difficult to understand. The groups should be a safe place to express these concerns.

- Groups can give opportunities for deep friendships to develop. Group members will be encouraged to talk about their experiences, feelings, questions, hopes and fears. They will be able to offer one another pastoral support and to be involved in each other's lives.

- There is a difference between being a collection of individuals who happen to meet together every Wednesday (or any day) and being an effective group who bounce ideas off each other, spark inspiration and creativity, pooling their talents and resources to create solutions together: one whose whole is definitely greater than the sum of its parts. The process of working through these studies will encourage healthy group dynamics.

Space is given for you to write answers, comments, questions and thoughts. This book will not tell you what to think, but it will help you discover the truth of God's word through thinking, discussing, praying and listening.

## FOR GROUP MEMBERS

- You will probably get more out of the study if you spend some time during the week reading the passage and thinking about the questions. Make a note of anything you don't understand.

- Pray that God will help you to understand the passage and show you how to apply it. Pray for other members in the group too, that they will find the study helpful.

- Be willing to take part in the discussions. The leader of the group is not there as an expert with all the answers. They will want everyone to get involved and share their thoughts and opinions.

- However, don't dominate the group! If you are aware that you are saying a lot, make space for others to contribute. Be sensitive to other group members and aim to be encouraging. If you disagree with someone, say so but without putting down their contribution.

## FOR INDIVIDUALS

- Although this book is written with a group in mind, it can also be easily used by individuals. You obviously won't be able to do the group activities suggested, but you can consider how you would answer the questions and write your thoughts in the space provided.

- You may find it helpful to talk to a prayer partner about what you have learnt, and ask them to pray for you as you try and apply what you are learning to your life.

# Introduction

> 'Jesus told them, "The harvest is plentiful, but the workers are few. Ask the Lord of the harvest, therefore, to send out workers into his harvest field."'
>
> *Luke 10:2*

In March 2015 more than 40 leaders of denominations and networks from across the spectrum of the UK Church gathered in the Lake District. For 24 hours, we prayed and we talked. We shared our heart for mission; our collective longing to see God move in this nation. We reflected on an initial piece of research into *People's Perceptions of Jesus, Christians and Evangelism* - we had commissioned the Barna Research Group to survey 1,000 people in England. The results of this first piece of research were shocking.

We agreed that this research had the potential to equip every Christian to have millions more sensitive, positive, culturally-relevant conversations about Jesus that could be deeply effective in evangelism. But we wanted to make sure. So denominational leaders agreed to fund further, more comprehensive, research – the results of which have been published in Talking Jesus – *www.talkingjesus.org*.

To give further depth to the research, ComRes interviewed 3,014 UK adults aged 18+ online during 12-23 July 2015. The data was weighted to be representative of all UK adults by age, gender, region and socio-economic grade. ComRes also interviewed 1,621 UK practising Christians online during 17-29 June 2015. The data was weighted to be representative of all UK practising Christians by age, gender and denomination as per the Church Census 2005. The ComRes data was analysed by Barna Research Group, who based their analysis on samples of 2,545 English adults and 1,592 practising Christians taken from the ComRes UK samples.

## LEADERS UNITE

There are rare moments in Church history where the unity of God's people is tangible. This was one of those moments. The leaders gathered for those 24 hours at Windermere agreed to work together toward 2050 on some key benchmarks: the number of people that know who Jesus is; the number of non-Christians who know a Christian; the number who have had a positive conversation with a Christian; and the percentage of the population who are practising Christians.

Now the real work has begun, and it began with prayer as churches throughout the UK launched 2016 using the Talking Jesus prayer resources. You can find these resources at **www.talkingjesus.org**. We need the Holy Spirit to be at work in our country. We need the Holy Spirit to use our words and actions to show people what Jesus is like. We need the Holy Spirit to give Christians the right words to say in every situation, and we need the Holy Spirit to draw people to Jesus.

The Talking Jesus research provokes us to prayer as our hearts are heavy with the reality of how little our friends and neighbours understand about who Jesus is. But there are glimmers of hope; we are excited about this unique opportunity to understand the landscape we are in. This is not a quick-fix strategy, but a long-term commitment to changing the story in our nation, so that people might meet Jesus, love him and follow him.

This study draws on the Talking Jesus research for the UK. The full findings, complete with graphs and charts, are available online at **www.talkingjesus.org**. Responding to these findings, we will look at the mission strategy of the early Church, calling us to pray for the people in our villages, towns and cities throughout the UK.

Talking and listening to our Father in prayer helps us to prepare the way for him to use us. As he changes us and fills us with his love and compassion, we find confidence to pray for others and share the Good News with those have not yet encountered Jesus.

We long to see our country transformed – let's encourage one another as together we seek to be game-changers in God's plan for the UK.

'May God be gracious to us and bless us and make his face shine upon us, that your ways may be known on earth, your salvation among all nations'

*Psalm 67:1-2*

**AIM: To discover what made the early Church grow.**

 **GAME**

Introductions – go round the room shaking hands with everyone and telling them each a bit of information about yourself: your favourite colour, food, film, hobby, piece of music etc.

 **STORY**

Jake and Michele's neighbours invited them to their daughter's christening, which was part of a Sunday morning church service. The couple only ever attended church for weddings and funerals, but they considered themselves to be quite spiritual. Michele had tried various healing therapies and one of Jake's tattoos was religious. They mixed easily with the other guests at the buffet lunch after the christening and Jake got talking to Steve, one of the church members; they had worked on the same building site a year earlier. Jake and Michele were intrigued by their first Sunday morning at church. The atmosphere was upbeat and positive – like a good night out at the local pub only no one was drinking – just singing, praying and listening to a talk. They met people they knew around town. They'd been to school with one or two of them. Michele's cousin was in the congregation. Their son's school teacher was on the team serving lunch. And two or three other neighbours were involved. They had loads of connections, but no one had ever talked to them about Jesus. Michele picked up an invitation to an Alpha supper as they left for home. She wanted to know what made these people tick. A year later and they had both become Christians and had been baptised. Ten years on and they are still following Jesus.

 **SCRIPTURE**

Read Acts 1:8 and 2:22-40

...you will receive power when the Holy Spirit comes on you; and you will be my witnesses in Jerusalem, and in all Judea and Samaria, and to the ends of the earth.

*Acts 1:8*

Fellow Israelites, listen to this: Jesus of Nazareth was a man accredited by God to you by miracles, wonders and signs, which God did among you through him, as you yourselves know. This man was handed over to you by God's deliberate plan and foreknowledge; and you, with the help of wicked men, put him to death by nailing him to the cross. But God raised him from the dead, freeing him from the agony of death, because it was impossible for death to keep its hold on him. David said about him:

> '"I saw the Lord always before me.
> Because he is at my right hand,
> I will not be shaken.
> Therefore my heart is glad and my tongue rejoices;
> my body also will rest in hope,
> because you will not abandon me to the realm of the dead,
> you will not let your holy one see decay.
> You have made known to me the paths of life;
> you will fill me with joy in your presence."

'Fellow Israelites, I can tell you confidently that the patriarch David died and was buried, and his tomb is here to this day. But he was a prophet and knew that God had promised him on oath that he would place one of his descendants on his throne. Seeing what was to come, he spoke of the resurrection of the Messiah, that he was not abandoned to the realm of the dead, nor did his body see decay. God has raised this Jesus to life, and we are all witnesses of it. Exalted to the right hand of God, he has received from the Father the promised Holy Spirit and has poured out what you now see and hear. For David did not ascend to heaven, and yet he said,

> '"The Lord said to my Lord:
> 'Sit at my right hand
> until I make your enemies
> a footstool for your feet.'"

'Therefore let all Israel be assured of this: God has made this Jesus, whom you crucified, both Lord and Messiah.'

When the people heard this, they were cut to the heart and said to Peter and the other apostles, 'Brothers, what shall we do?'

Peter replied, 'Repent and be baptised, every one of you, in the name of Jesus Christ for the forgiveness of your sins. And you will receive the gift of the Holy Spirit. The promise is for you and your children and for all who are far off – for all whom the Lord our God will call.'

With many other words he warned them; and he pleaded with them, 'Save yourselves from this corrupt generation.' Those who accepted his message were baptised, and about three thousand were added to their number that day.

*Acts 2:22-40*

#  TALKING JESUS

Family and friends are key to people finding faith for themselves in modern Britain. According to the Talking Jesus research, a majority of non-Christians in the UK know a Christian. Nearly seven in ten non-Christians report that they personally know someone who is a follower of Jesus—that is, someone they perceive to be a 'practising Christian' (68%). This is amazing – particularly as most of these Christians are either family members (35%) or friends (38%).

However, one in three UK adults do not know a practising Christian (33%). These individuals are more likely than average to be under the age of 35 (39%), ages 35-44 (24%), Asian or Asian British (9%)—specifically Pakistani (3%) or Indian (3%).

#  WHAT IS YOUR REFLECTION

How did the first 3,000 Christians find out about Jesus?

How did Peter talk about Jesus?

What helped those people in Jerusalem to become Jesus' followers?

Who are your friends and family, who know that you are a Christian, but who are not yet followers of Jesus themselves?

Who do you know, who is under the age of 35, who might not know that you are a follower of Jesus?

**My thoughts and notes....**

# 💬 OUR REFLECTION

Pentecost changed everything for Jesus' followers. The power of God, that had raised Jesus from the dead, was poured out on them and they were transformed. Peter was a prime example. When Jesus was arrested, Peter had denied even knowing him. Now, we see this rough, unschooled fisherman, empowered by the Holy Spirit, speaking boldly with confidence to the crowds gathered in Jerusalem. His focus is Jesus, his death and resurrection. He knows his audience and speaks into their situation giving Jesus a historical and geographical context, linking him to King David, one of the crowd's heroes.

From the small group of believers – about 120 (Acts 1:15), the Church grew to more than 3,000 following one sermon. The Good News then travelled from Jerusalem, throughout the region, to Europe, Asia and Africa. Jews and Gentiles heard about Jesus and followed him: men and women, slave and free.

God had chosen a strategic time and place to birth the Church. There were people of every nationality in Jerusalem, gathered for a major Jewish festival. Many heard the Good News about Jesus and the impact was amazing.

Luke's account of the early Church is a story of growth.

'And the Lord added to their number daily those who were being saved.'

*Acts 2:47*

'But many who heard the message believed; so the number of men who believed grew to about five thousand.'

*Acts 4:4*

'So the word of God spread. The number of disciples in Jerusalem increased rapidly, and a large number of priests became obedient to the faith.'

*Acts 6:7*

'Then the church throughout Judea, Galilee and Samaria enjoyed a time of peace and was strengthened. Living in the fear of the Lord and encouraged by the Holy Spirit, it increased in numbers.'

*Acts 9:31*

'But the word of God continued to spread and flourish.'

*Acts 12:24*

'So the churches were strengthened in the faith and grew daily in numbers.'

*Acts 16:5*

'In this way the word of the Lord spread widely and grew in power.'

*Acts 19:20*

'He proclaimed the kingdom of God and taught about the Lord Jesus Christ – with all boldness and without hindrance!'

*Acts 28:31*

The early Church spent time together for teaching, fellowship, meals and prayer. They cared for each other and people could see that lives were being transformed. Proclamation of the gospel went alongside incarnation and transformation. When Peter proclaimed the Good News, people responded. Our churches probably have similar elements, so what's different?

If you look at the religious news making headlines, you'll rarely find a story about Jesus. Do we make the main thing, THE main thing in our conversations? Does Jesus ever get a mention?

One thing to note is the different ways we communicate when our encounters with people are passing or permanent. In our permanent relationships with friends and family we need to be sensitive to God's guidance when we talk about Jesus – drip-feeding not drowning; and through actions as well as words.

**My thoughts and notes....**

In the Talking Jesus research, practising Christians were asked how they came to faith. Conversations and relationships with family and friends were crucial. Christian leaders, vicars and ministers were reported as having a much less significant role in the process. We can draw a very simple conclusion from this. If we want to see more of our nation impacted by the Christian message, then we need to equip as many Christians as possible to 'be prepared to give an answer to everyone who asks you to give the reason for the hope that you have. But do this with gentleness and respect...' (1 Peter 3:15).

 ## KEY THOUGHT

Jesus promised '...you will receive power when the Holy Spirit comes on you; and you will be my witnesses'. This isn't a tentative suggestion but a confident assertion. As followers of Jesus we are empowered by the Holy Spirit and we are *his* witnesses – witnesses to Jesus.

 ## APPLICATION

What was the focus of the early Church?

What is the focus of our church life?

How did you first find out about Jesus?

What helped you to become a Christian?

Describe the last opportunity you had to talk to someone about Jesus.

What has been effective in helping the people you meet to discover Jesus for themselves?

# ✓ ACTION PLAN

Take turns to tell your story – how you became a Christian.

Thinking about your friends, family and other people you meet – particularly those under 35 – what might happen if you mention Jesus to them this coming week?

# 🔥 PRAYER

Spend time thanking God for the people who were part of your journey to faith. Pray for the people you meet who don't yet know Jesus. Ask God for an opportunity in the coming week to talk to them about Jesus in a natural, not pushy, way – with 'gentleness and respect'.

# Session 2: The nature of the change

 ## AIM: To refocus on THE main thing

 ## GAME

Look at some pictures, printed or on a screen, prepared in advance. (See Leader's notes for guidance.) What do you see when you look at these pictures? Sometimes we need to see things from a different perspective.

 ## STORY

Sara grew up in a Christian family. At Sunday school, creative and dedicated teachers told her the Bible stories that she also heard at home from her parents. As a teenager she was part of a lively youth group. She made a personal commitment to Christ. But when her peer group split up to go to university, Sara began to drift away. University was her chance to escape her Christian upbringing – or so she thought. When a friend asked her for Sunday lunch after church one week, she went to the morning service. Just for one week, she thought. That Sunday the sermon ended with an appeal. It was as if everything that had been said was directed at her. She had to respond. The couple who spoke with her at the altar listened to some of her story: 'I've heard all this before. It works for other people, but not for me,' she said.

'Spend the next week reading one of the gospels. Find out about Jesus,' the couple said. 'You read; we'll pray. Come back next week and talk to us again.'

That week she read Matthew's gospel. It was as if she had never heard of Jesus before. She saw him with fresh eyes and responded to his love, forgiveness and offer of a fresh start. Three decades later she is still following him.

 ## SCRIPTURE

When Peter saw this, he said to them: 'Fellow Israelites, why does this surprise you? Why do you stare at us as if by our own power or godliness we had made this man walk? The God of Abraham, Isaac and Jacob, the God of our fathers, has glorified his servant Jesus. You handed him over to be killed, and you disowned him before Pilate, though he had decided to let him go. You disowned the Holy and Righteous One and asked that a murderer be released to you. You killed the author of life, but God raised him from the dead. We are witnesses of this. By faith in the name of Jesus, this man whom you see and know was made strong. It is Jesus' name and the faith that comes through him that has completely healed him, as you can all see.

'Now, fellow Israelites, I know that you acted in ignorance, as did your leaders. But this is how God fulfilled what he had foretold through all the prophets, saying that his Messiah would suffer. Repent, then, and turn to God, so that your sins may be wiped out, that times of refreshing may come from the Lord, and that he may send the Messiah, who has been appointed for you – even Jesus. Heaven must receive him until the time comes for God to restore everything, as he promised long ago through his holy prophets.

*Acts 3:12-21*

The priests and the captain of the temple guard and the Sadducees came up to Peter and John while they were speaking to the people. They were greatly disturbed because the apostles were teaching the people, proclaiming in Jesus the resurrection of the dead. They seized Peter and John and, because it was evening, they put them in jail until the next day. But many who heard the message believed; so the number of men who believed grew to about five thousand.

The next day the rulers, the elders and the teachers of the law met in Jerusalem. Annas the high priest was there, and so were Caiaphas, John, Alexander and others of the high priest's family. They had Peter and John brought before them and began to question them: 'By what power or what name did you do this?'

Then Peter, filled with the Holy Spirit, said to them: 'Rulers and elders of the people! If we are being called to account today for an act of kindness shown to a man who was lame and are being asked how he was healed, then know this, you and all the people of Israel: it is by the name of Jesus Christ of Nazareth, whom you crucified but whom God raised from the dead, that this man stands before you healed. Jesus is

'"the stone you builders rejected,

which has become the cornerstone."

Salvation is found in no one else, for there is no other name under heaven given to mankind by which we must be saved.'

*Acts 4:1-12*

 **TALKING JESUS**

Key facts:

- 61% of UK adults believe Jesus was a real person.

- 22% of UK adults hold the orthodox belief that Jesus was 'God in human form who lived among people in the first Century'.

- 44% of UK adults believe in the resurrection of Jesus from the dead.

The Talking Jesus research asked people: 'Which of the following best describes your understanding of Jesus Christ?'

Six in ten UK adults believe Jesus was a real person. Adults 35 and older are more likely than those 18 to 34 to believe Jesus actually lived. Conversely, younger adults are more likely than those over 35 to believe Jesus was a 'fictional character from a book and not a real, historical person'. More than two fifths of UK adults who are not practising Christians either do not believe Jesus was a real person who actually lived, or they are unsure if he was real or not.

Belief in Jesus' divinity is not common. Only about one in five UK adults holds the orthodox belief that Jesus was 'God in human form who lived among people in the first Century' (22%). The most common belief about Jesus is that he was 'a prophet or spiritual leader, not God' (29%).

Most ethnic minorities believe Jesus was a real person but are divided on whether or not he is God. Four out of five believe 'Jesus was a real person who actually lived' (79%), but only 25% believe Jesus was 'God in human form'.

Just under half of UK adults believe in the resurrection of Jesus from the dead (44%). One in six believe 'the resurrection happened word-for-word as described in the Bible' (17%) while one-quarter believe the biblical story 'contains some content which should not be taken literally' (26%).

As you can see, people don't necessarily think logically: 44% believe Jesus rose from the dead, but only 22% think he was God in human form. Some people do want facts and evidence, but many people respond to Jesus without thinking about history or archaeology. For most people, it's the impact of Jesus in people's lives today that makes the difference. Being able to tell your own story is more important than being able to recite facts from history. If necessary, you can point enquirers to ***bethinking.org*** for a wide range of videos discussing the facts of Jesus' life, death and resurrection.

For those who need to know, what are the facts about Jesus? Dr James Carleton-Paget, senior lecturer in New Testament Studies at Cambridge University, told the Talking Jesus report team: 'The argument that Jesus never existed, which has had a number of advocates since the 19th century, was not one that the enemies of Christianity in the ancient world ever used. While technically, we shall never be able to prove that Jesus existed, the real difficulty with arguing that he did not lies in explaining how it was that the central character of the New Testament was dreamed up by those who became his followers. The tale of a crucified Jewish saviour, in spite of arguments to the contrary, is simply too unlikely, even outrageous a story, to have had its origins in no more than the frenzied imaginations of a group of ordinary Galilean Jews.'

So, can we rely on the biblical account of Jesus' life, death and resurrection? According to Dr Peter J. Williams, Chair of the International Greek New Testament Project and Warden of Tyndale House, which is dedicated to researching all the primary evidence relevant to the study of the Bible: 'The manuscript evidence for Mark's gospel is far better than that of most classical works, even though there are fewer early copies of Mark's gospel than of the other gospels (Matthew, Luke, and John). The earliest extensive copy of Mark's gospel is probably the manuscript of all four gospels known as P45 and held in Dublin. It is generally dated to around AD 225. The gap between the time of composition of a piece of classical Latin or Greek literature and the earliest extensive copy is usually much greater than for Mark, and yet classical scholars accept the basic reliability of the text as transmitted in later manuscripts. However, there are also indications that Mark's gospel was in continuous use among Christians from the time it was written to the time of our earliest copy.'[1]

#  WHAT IS YOUR REFLECTION?

What are the specific claims Peter makes about Jesus?

How did he explain who Jesus is and why he lived?

What was the source of Peter's confidence?

How is a one-off encounter different from an on-going relationship when we are talking about Jesus?

Looking back to the last session, how has God opened up opportunities for you to talk about Jesus with the people you prayed about?

**My thoughts and notes....**

---

1    http://www.theologynetwork.org/biblical-studies/the-historical-reliability-of-marks-gospel.htm

# OUR REFLECTION

Peter pulls no punches in his preaching! With a couple of quick questions, he shifts the focus from a miraculous healing onto Jesus. In Peter's eyes the miracle serves only to glorify Jesus. Peter's message still rings true today: Christ has died; Christ is risen; Christ will come again! His words were like a red rag to a bull for this particular audience. Sadducees were a small but powerful Jewish sect who did not believe in the resurrection of the dead. Peter calls for a response from them: Repent... turn to God.

Again, in chapter 4, Peter brings the focus onto Jesus, with the blunt assertion: 'Salvation is found in no one else...' It was enough to get them jailed again, especially when Peter and John tell their accusers: 'We cannot help speaking about what we have seen and heard.'

When they are released they head straight to where the church is meeting to pray and worship. Most of us would have thanked God for a safe return and prayed for protection. Not Peter and John. Praising God for his sovereignty, they ask for boldness to speak about Jesus and they invite God to follow up their words with miraculous signs.

Already they know that the good news isn't just for their small gatherings in home groups; this good news is for everyone. And they know that opposition is part of the package for Jesus' followers.

Acts 4 ends with a brief summary of their values and way of life. They are united – 'one in heart and mind'. Their actions and words testify to Jesus and there's no division between sacred and secular – their whole lives are devoted to God.

Peter speaks with the conviction of an eye-witness: 'God has raised this Jesus to life: and we are all witnesses of the fact' (2:32) ... 'God raised him from the dead. We are witnesses of this' (3:15). As we go through Acts we meet other game-changers, like Paul, who were not eye-witnesses to Jesus' life, death and resurrection, but whose lives were also transformed by their encounter with the risen Lord Jesus.

Peter and John's opportunity to speak about Jesus in this example came from a lame man's longing. He wanted something from them and, rather than money, they gave him a fresh start in life. Some people respond to Jesus because of a logical process: 'Jesus was a real person who lived, died and rose again. I need to respond.' Many people respond because Jesus meets them at their point of need, and when they see and hear how Jesus has changed other people's lives.

The Talking Jesus report found that when Christians have a conversation about Jesus one in five of those they talk to want to 'experience the love of Jesus Christ for themselves' (20%) or 'request prayer on behalf of themselves, or a friend or family member' (19%). Nearly as many say 'they are looking into Christianity more broadly' (18%), while others 'express an interest in going to church' (17%); 'ask to have another conversation' about Jesus (10%); or ask how they could 'find out more about Jesus' (6%).

#  KEY THOUGHT

Peter and John told their accusers 'we cannot help speaking about what we have seen and heard'. The impact of Jesus was plain to see in their own lives and in the lives of people around them.

 # APPLICATION

How do you explain who Jesus is and why he lived?

How confident are you in the biblical account of Jesus' life, death and resurrection?

What have you seen and heard of Jesus' impact in people's lives?

How do you feel in conversations about faith?

Are there points you avoid making, depending on who you are talking to?

Visit *focus.org.uk* and watch the five-minute video 'Was Jesus a real person?' to see historians and theologians tracing evidence from non-Christian sources.

 # ACTION PLAN

Think back to the last session, and the people you prayed for, think about their needs. What are they looking for in life? What could you do to help meet their needs?

List the questions you have been asked about your faith.

What question might be the game-changer. What could you ask which could provoke awareness of a hunger for the life Jesus offers?

Choose two people to role-play a discussion where one person is asking about Jesus and the other is responding.

Thinking about the different groups of people you are praying for, what are the different aspects of the gospel which meet them at their different points of need?

# PRAYER

List the names of the people you meet regularly who don't yet know Jesus. Pray together for the top five by name, asking God to give you natural opportunities to respond practically to their needs and talk to them about Jesus. Ask God for boldness, wisdom and sensitivity.

# Session 3: Your change

 ## AIM: Hearts and minds transformed

 ## GAME

Bridge building – divide into two teams and have a competition to build a bridge over one of the team members using newspaper and sticky tape.

 ## STORY

On a cold May morning, a young preacher wakes up in his tent to discover that his £50 sleeping bag is not fit for purpose. The colder he gets, the more he reflects that the weekend he is spending with 15 young people is a waste of time. They're not interested in the Christian story, and as he mulls this, the young preacher turns into the famous Dastardly side-kick Muttley and begins to whinge and moan. He directs some of this in prayer to God, and asks: 'Why am I here?'

To his surprise, he senses God asking him: 'What do you see?' and he tells the Lord that he sees disinterested, bored young people. As he explains this, he feels God start to respond, telling him that each young person is incredibly valued and loved by his heavenly Father. In this moment, the young man discovers that not only is his sleeping bag not fit for purpose; neither is his heart. He cries out to God to change his heart. That day, the young people respond in an amazing and extraordinary way to his preaching.

 ## SCRIPTURE

About noon the following day as they were on their journey and approaching the city, Peter went up on the roof to pray. He became hungry and wanted something to eat, and while the meal was being prepared, he fell into a trance. He saw heaven opened and something like a large sheet being let down to earth by its four corners. It contained all kinds of four-footed animals, as well as reptiles and birds. Then a voice told him, 'Get up, Peter. Kill and eat.' 'Surely not, Lord!' Peter replied. 'I have never eaten anything impure or unclean.'

The voice spoke to him a second time, 'Do not call anything impure that God has made clean.'

*Acts 10:9-15*

Then Peter began to speak: 'I now realise how true it is that God does not show favouritism but accepts from every nation the one who fears him and does what is right. You know the message God sent to the people of Israel, announcing the good news of peace through Jesus Christ, who is Lord of all. You know what has happened throughout the province of Judea, beginning in Galilee after the baptism that John preached – how God anointed Jesus of Nazareth with the Holy Spirit and power, and how he went around doing good and healing all who were under the power of the devil, because God was with him.

'We are witnesses of everything he did in the country of the Jews and in Jerusalem. They killed him by hanging him on a cross, but God raised him from the dead on the third day and caused him to be seen. He was not seen by all the people, but by witnesses whom God had already chosen – by us who ate and drank with him after he rose from the dead. He commanded us to preach to the people and to testify that he is the one whom God appointed as judge of the living and the dead. All the prophets testify about him that everyone who believes in him receives forgiveness of sins through his name.'

While Peter was still speaking these words, the Holy Spirit came on all who heard the message. The circumcised believers who had come with Peter were astonished that the gift of the Holy Spirit had been poured out even on Gentiles. For they heard them speaking in tongues and praising God.

Then Peter said, 'Surely no one can stand in the way of their being baptised with water. They have received the Holy Spirit just as we have.' So he ordered that they be baptised in the name of Jesus Christ. Then they asked Peter to stay with them for a few days.

*Acts 10: 34-48*

# TALKING JESUS

UK practising Christians feel a responsibility to evangelise (85%). Nearly half *strongly agree* that 'it is every Christian's responsibility to talk to non-Christians about Jesus Christ' (46%), and another two in five *tend to agree* (39%). About one out of ten say they *tend to disagree* with the statement (10%).

Most practising Christians have recently talked about Jesus with a non-Christian. Two-thirds have talked about their faith in Jesus within the past month (66%). Eight in ten have talked with a non-Christian about Jesus in the past six months (81%).

Most practising Christians feel confident to talk with non-Christians about Jesus (71%). A significant minority are 'afraid of causing offence when talking to non-Christians' (32%); think others are better suited to talking with non-Christians about Jesus (36%); or 'do not know how to talk to non-Christians about Jesus' (24%).

Younger Christians talk about Jesus with non-Christians more often than do older Christians. Nearly twice as many young adults aged 18 to 34 (practising and non-practising combined) say they talked about their relationship with Jesus in the past month (33%) compared to adults 35 and older (18%). Younger adults most often talked about Jesus with friends and family.

When Christians talk about Jesus, the response is mixed. One in five non-Christians say, after such a conversation, they felt open to an experience or encounter with Jesus; 19% ask for prayer for themselves, or a friend or family member; 18% say they are looking into Christianity more broadly; 17% express an interest in going to church.

#  WHAT IS YOUR REFLECTION?

How did God intervene in Peter's life?

What do you think Peter's vision meant?

What were the obstacles to be overcome in the meeting between Cornelius and Peter?

What was the impact of the meeting?

Thinking about the people you have been praying for between sessions, have you made assumptions about how they might respond to Jesus?

Are there people who you wouldn't bother talking to about Jesus, because you don't expect them to be interested?

**My thoughts and notes....**

# OUR REFLECTION

This scripture highlights how Peter discovered that his heart and worldview were not fit for purpose. A game-changing vision gave him a new way to live.

Peter already knew in theory that the Christian message was for all people and for all nations. He had heard Jesus tell him and the rest of the disciples, as recorded in Matthew 28:19 'Therefore go and make disciples of all nations.' Peter, like many of us, was trying to obey the commands of Christ as he understood them, but his background - his strict Jewish upbringing - stopped him seeing the full dynamic of what God had in mind. In this story he discovers God's perspective on 'all nations'; God means literally everybody.

As the messengers came from the household of Cornelius, Peter rises up to respond to them and he goes with them. This is not just a physical thing. His heart had changed and therefore his reactions to his world were changing. He stepped out into relationships that he would not have done up until that moment.

In many ways, we are like Peter. We compartmentalise our lives and limit our understanding of mission. We have blind spots that limit our expectations of what God can do. We can tend to 'do mission' and only reach out when we are pushed; and when there are new ideas. The challenge is to embrace a missional lifestyle so that mission is part of our daily lives; something that is appropriate all day, every day. For this to happen, we need a fresh encounter with Jesus: to see his heart; to know that he died for all – and that everybody has value. We need to ask God for big hearts to discover that God loves all the people we meet. That's the basis for us to reach out.

The Talking Jesus research gives a very interesting picture of how adults in the nation view Jesus Christ. As we learned in the last session, the good news is that one in five want to know more about our Christian faith.

 # KEY THOUGHT

Peter's heart and mind were transformed as he began to understand God's radical inclusivity: 'I now realise how true it is that God does not show favouritism but accepts from every nation the one who fears him and does what is right.'

 # APPLICATION

Recognise your blind spots. Who are the people you think are beyond God's reach? People who couldn't become Christians?

Who are the unreached people in your community?

How does prejudice limit the spread of the gospel today?

To what extent are the people in your church fully mobilised?

Does your church take seriously the challenge to 'Go!' or is your mission focused on inviting people to come in?

What hinders us going out of our comfort zones and being more actively involved in faith-sharing?

Recall the last time you spoke about Jesus to someone who is not a Christian. How did the conversation start? What was the impact?

How can we support each other and encourage mission as a lifestyle? Draw up a list of ideas for your group.

Think about the mission opportunities presented by initiatives like Street Pastors, Foodbanks, Night Shelters, CAP debt advice groups and other practical projects which serve communities. Consider how you can support these groups locally.

 **ACTION PLAN**

Game-changers need changed hearts. Pray for each other, that each person in the group will have a fresh encounter with Jesus. Our change comes first.

Feedback on what has happened since you last met; what opportunities have there been to respond to the needs of the people you are praying for?

Take encouragement from the fact that one in five of the people we talk to about Jesus is interested in finding out more.

Pray by name for the five people you have listed in previous sessions. Does your list need revising in the light of this session's study on Peter's changed heart?

 **PRAYER**

Acts 1:8 is the promise of Jesus that the power of the Holy Spirit will come upon us and we will be his witnesses. The root of the word 'witness' is the word 'martyr'. To witness is to lay our lives down or, as a Salvation Army officer once said, 'It is the power to love like Jesus loves.' So let us pray for one another and our churches, for the power of the Holy Spirit to enable us to love like Jesus loves and to reach out.

**AIM: For us all to be equipped for mission in our words, deeds and values.**

 **GAME**

What's my line? Put stickers on people's backs with different job titles. Everyone mixes and asks questions about their job role, until they can guess their job title.

 **STORY**

A young preacher had an opportunity to speak to a group of Christian lawyers in London with a view to recruiting them for the mission field. In his mind, their work had little value or importance. His work was the 'real thing', or so he thought. But as he prepared the talk, the script that developed was not what he had originally planned. As a result, he came to understand and was able to tell the lawyers that they were already as much missionaries as he was. They were called to live out Christian values; to value people; and to do their work in the light of Christian principles. As their work would be more about the transforming impact of Christ in them over a long period of time, for some of them it would be very hard to measure the impact. But they needed to be confident that their active presence was making a difference. He told them that the challenge for Christians in the work place is to go from being passive to active; actively bringing Christian values into every day. It's these values that make a difference. This would make their work far more challenging than the young preacher's, as he could see the impact he had on young people as he spoke to them. The lawyers had to trust God and leave the impact of their lives in his hands.

At the end of the meeting, to the surprise of the young preacher, there was an awkward silence. Several of the young lawyers were crying. They said 'Thank you. You have told us that we are not second-class Christians. We're first class, and God has a purpose for us where we work, where we live, and in our communities.'

#  SCRIPTURE

From Troas we put out to sea and sailed straight for Samothrace, and the next day we went on to Neapolis. From there we travelled to Philippi, a Roman colony and the leading city of that district of Macedonia. And we stayed there several days.

On the Sabbath we went outside the city gate to the river, where we expected to find a place of prayer. We sat down and began to speak to the women who had gathered there. One of those listening was a woman from the city of Thyatira named Lydia, a dealer in purple cloth. She was a worshipper of God. The Lord opened her heart to respond to Paul's message. When she and the members of her household were baptised, she invited us to her home. 'If you consider me a believer in the Lord,' she said, 'come and stay at my house.' And she persuaded us.

*Acts 16:11-15*

#  TALKING JESUS

When Christians talk about Jesus, the response is mixed. One in five non-Christians say that after such a conversation, they felt open to an experience or encounter with Jesus. But around half say they were not open to such an experience and didn't want to know more about Jesus. One in six did want to know more (18%); 16% felt sad that they did not share the Christian's faith; nearly one-quarter felt more positive about Jesus (22%) or felt closer to the Christian with whom they had the conversation (27%).

More than half of UK non-Christians who know a Christian (57%) have had a conversation with them about Jesus. Younger adults 18 to 34 are somewhat more likely than adults over 35 to report having had such a conversation. Two out of every five non-Christians say evangelism made them glad not to be a Christian (43%). Another two in five don't know how they felt about it (41%), while 16% felt sad, after the conversation about Jesus, that they did not share the Christian's faith.

#  WHAT IS YOUR REFLECTION?

What does Luke tell us about Lydia? Who might be a modern equivalent?

What's the catalyst to change in Lydia's life?

What were the implications of her invitation to Peter?

**My thoughts and notes....**

Thinking about the conversations you have had with non-Christians, what was their response?

Talk about the conversations you have had with people on your prayer list, since you last met. What opportunities have you had to talk about Jesus?

 **OUR REFLECTION**

When you read the book of Acts, at first glance, it all looks a little random, and that there was no coherent strategy on how the early church would reach the Roman Empire and beyond. But as you look closer into the ministry of the Apostle Paul, you begin to see a very clear and simple strategy. Paul understands who are the right people to reach in each of the communities he goes to. His strategy was to find the people who were open, and go to them first. Then, as they found faith, they would be able to take the challenge of reaching the wider community. Obviously, if Paul was in a place for a longer time, he could not only reach the open group, but also those who understood very little about Christianity.

So what was the pattern? Firstly, Paul goes to Jews where they are. He saw them as open people, despite the fact that some turned against him, because they would understand his language and his biblical references. He reaped a harvest. So for us, this equates to the 61% who do believe that Jesus was a real person who actually lived, especially the 44% who do believe in the resurrection. We need to tune our hearts and our minds to identify who these people are. This will often be demonstrated by their positive response to us; the questions they ask; the fact they want to know more; their openness to going to events such as carol services or Alpha courses.

The second group of people that the Apostle Paul went to are people like Lydia. He looked for people who were pagan, not Jewish, who had a spiritual hunger. There were laws in Philippi stopping people practising unrecognised religions in the city, so people like Lydia prayed outside the city gate. Paul looked for this place of prayer and went to them. Gender wasn't a boundary for Paul. Lydia responds very positively.

 # KEY THOUGHT

'The Lord opened her heart to respond to Paul's message.' We need to meet people where they are. But, even if we are in the right place at the right time, the outcome is in God's hands.

 # APPLICATION

Think about your community. Where do people meet who are interested in spiritual matters, but aren't Christians? In *Sowing, Reaping, Keeping*[2] , Laurence Singlehurst, tells us that all relationships are made in the context of doing something: sport, evening classes, charity work, hobbies... This context enables us to build relationships; to demonstrate our faith by the way we live, and to speak about it as the appropriate moment arises.

The underlying challenge for the church is to realise that people are not going to come to us. The attractional model of mission will not change the nation. The Apostle Paul went to the people and engaged with them where they were. We must go and engage with people in ways that are appropriate to our community. What might that look like?

There might be some pressing needs in our community. In the last ten years we have seen how projects such as Foodbanks, CAP debt advice centres and Street Pastors, meet people's needs

2   Find details in Recommended Resources list at the back.

and create a context of care and unconditional love. This has reconnected churches with people in their neighbourhoods and has made a huge difference as we seek to love and serve our community, regardless of whether they respond or not.

Everyday life also offers opportunities. We have already seen the significance of family and friendship. But also, there is the challenge of just being a good neighbour. Do we know the names and the needs of the people who live beside us, above us, below us? There is the impact of the school gate. Many lasting friendships are made between parents at the school gate. This amazing context creates ongoing opportunities for relationships and friendships. Out of these, there is always a percentage of people finding faith.

We need to move from an attractional model of church to a missional model. Friendships made through projects, parent and toddler groups, hobbies, and sports are contexts to live out and speak about our faith. Through these, like the apostle Paul, we have a strategy to introduce people to Jesus.

##  ACTION PLAN

Where do you meet people who are not Christians?

What are your principles for faith-living and faith-sharing where you work and live?

HOPE, a charity that exists to bring churches together in mission, provides a Fun-size Mission Academy that has been used by hundreds of young people as they develop a lifestyle of mission. They use a 'Chatterbox' to ask four short, challenging questions:

1. Who – do we want to reach?

2. What – are we going to do?

3. How – do we want to do it?

4. So – what have we learned?

Is there something specific you could do as a group to share Jesus' love with people who don't yet know Jesus? You could use the Chatterbox questions to make a plan.

Find out more on the HOPE website at **hopetogether.org.uk**

HOPE encourages churches to make the most of the Christian calendar as a basis for an ongoing rhythm of mission through the year. What might that look like in your area? Could you commit to 40 acts of kindness during Lent – and be ready to give a reason why? At Easter, might a shoe-shine stall in your local shopping precinct prompt questions that could point to Jesus who washed his disciples' feet? An Easter-egg give-away, hot cross buns for commuters, a car wash... activities like these could give opportunities for a pithy pointer to the Easter story. Christmas brings the prospect of carol singing, mince pie give-aways and many more ways to bless local people and point to Jesus.

 **PRAYER**

Pray for your neighbours or those in your close network by name. Ask God to help you to be sensitive to their needs and to give you the grace to serve them, even if relationships are not easy. Go on praying for the five people on your list. And be ready to feedback at the next session on how God is answering your prayers.

**AIM: To share the Christian story in language and metaphors that are shaped by the hearers.**

 **GAME**

Talk Time – divide into two teams and choose three household items for each team. Now use each item as an illustration to explain the Good News. You have one minute per item.

 **STORY**

A street chaplain was describing his work. Over a period of years, he has created relationships with people on a particular street. He seeks to understand their needs. He tells them he represents a number of churches in the area. As he does his work he finds that behind every door is a fresh challenge of language.

At Door 1 there is an elderly lady in her eighties who went to Sunday school when she was young. She even attended church a long time ago, so she understands Christian language. The chaplain can talk to her in the language of church, the language that he is most familiar with.

At Door 2 is a young mum. She is 30 years old and has never been to church; never been to Sunday school; knows nothing about Jesus, and wonders if he might be fiction. At this door, a whole new language is required. The street chaplain has to use vocabulary and metaphors that, to start with are strange to him, to relate faith to things that are happening in her world. She has experienced a lot of other people's selfishness. He talks about selfishness and how God wants to change our hearts.

At Door 3 is a young lady from a Hindu background. She was born in England, but knows very little about Jesus. This conversation needs another set of metaphors and vocabulary to communicate effectively.

 # SCRIPTURE

Paul then stood up in the meeting of the Areopagus and said: 'People of Athens! I see that in every way you are very religious. For as I walked around and looked carefully at your objects of worship, I even found an altar with this inscription: to an unknown god. So you are ignorant of the very thing you worship – and this is what I am going to proclaim to you.

'The God who made the world and everything in it is the Lord of heaven and earth and does not live in temples built by human hands. And he is not served by human hands, as if he needed anything. Rather, he himself gives everyone life and breath and everything else. From one man he made all the nations, that they should inhabit the whole earth; and he marked out their appointed times in history and the boundaries of their lands. God did this so that they would seek him and perhaps reach out for him and find him, though he is not far from any one of us. "For in him we live and move and have our being." As some of your own poets have said, "We are his offspring."

Therefore since we are God's offspring, we should not think that the divine being is like gold or silver or stone – an image made by human design and skill. In the past God overlooked such ignorance, but now he commands all people everywhere to repent. For he has set a day when he will judge the world with justice by the man he has appointed. He has given proof of this to everyone by raising him from the dead.'

When they heard about the resurrection of the dead, some of them sneered, but others said, 'We want to hear you again on this subject.' At that, Paul left the Council. Some of the people became followers of Paul and believed. Among them was Dionysius, a member of the Areopagus, also a woman named Damaris, and a number of others.

*Acts 17:22-34*

 # TALKING JESUS

The majority of UK non-Christians know a Christian who is either a family member (35%) or friend (38%). Nearly seven in ten non-Christians report that they personally know someone who is a follower of Jesus—that is, someone they perceive to be a 'practising Christian'.

Most non-Christians enjoy the company of the Christian they know (61%). Three out of five say they enjoy being around their Christian friend or family member always (28%) or most of the time (33%).

Non-Christians attribute more positive than negative qualities to the Christian they know. The most common positive perceptions are friendly (64%), caring (52%) and good-humoured (46%), while the most common negative perceptions include narrow-minded (13%), hypocritical (10%), and uptight (7%).

#  WHAT IS YOUR REFLECTION?

**My thoughts and notes....**

How was Paul's sermon different from Peter's (Acts 3:12-31, which we studied in session two)? Look particularly at the starting point of what Paul says.

In what ways does Paul relate to his audience?

What key points does Paul make about Jesus?

Feedback on any conversations you have had with people on your prayer list since the last session.

#  OUR REFLECTION

In the book of Acts, there are two big preaching stories. One is Peter preaching to the crowds at Pentecost (Acts 2:14-41) and then there is this account of Paul speaking to the crowds at the Aeropagus. We see two totally different sorts of language. Peter is talking to Jews who understand something of their own culture and story. His language is shaped by that. Paul speaks to people who are not Jews, who don't understand Christian language, so he uses language and metaphors drawn from their culture, even quoting their poets and an inscription from a statue of one of their gods. Paul addresses them in language they understand.

The story of the street chaplain that we read earlier, is the story of our lives too. In our multi-faith, multi-cultural nation, there is not one set of languages. We have to learn how to express faith in different ways, to share the Christian story with appropriate language and metaphors.

In the Talking Jesus research, a key statistic shows that 68% of our population knows a Christian. Most describe Christians in positive terms. Only a very small percentage see us in a negative way. That's good news. But 43% felt glad that they did not share our faith.

There are different ways to look at this statistic. One way is to say we have a language challenge. Even though we as Christians can be quite enthusiastic in sharing our faith, it would appear that it is not always helpful to the hearers.

In Acts, the response to Paul's message is that they would like to come back to talk again. This is a most encouraging and appropriate response in this context and in our own. The parable of the sower (Matthew 13:1-23) highlights the importance of understanding; that real faith comes from understanding. To understand the Christian gospel, many people need to talk more.

One significant development in the last 30 years has been Alpha, Christianity Explored and similar enquirers' courses. They demonstrate the Aeropagus dynamic – that over a period of time, in a safe environment, people get an opportunity to talk again. Luis Palau was one of the first evangelists in modern times to realise the importance of friendship, and of creating opportunities for people to talk again. Now, many evangelists have two altar calls. They share the Christian message and they invite people to Alpha or Christianity Explored, to talk about what they have heard. At the end of their message, these evangelists give a second altar call: 'There are some of you who have been around Christians, who do understand, and who would like to respond tonight.' This is more like Peter at Pentecost. In that situation, Peter understood that he was talking to people who had background knowledge; they knew enough to respond then and there. So Peter immediately jumps to the strong invitation and invites people to come to faith. Many respond.

Our culture is one where the majority of people don't have any background to the gospel. So we have to engage with what we could call 'conversational tennis' - always leaving people open to come back to us again. In other words, we are leaving people open for that next Holy Spirit encounter, trying to make sure that the words and the metaphors that we use are not religious clichés, but they have meaning in today's culture.

Different age groups need different approaches. Sean Dunne works with local churches in the Dallas / Fort Worth area of the USA. According to Dunne, most unchurched Millennials don't get up each day thinking about God or eternity. Instead they think about their challenges and their struggles. They don't connect Jesus or Christianity to their needs - this, according to Dunne, is why they need a media interruption. His media strategy is as follows: 'Instead of offering them an invitation that they can reject, we interrupt their media with messages of hope. Millennials are tired of the monologue they perceive from the church, but they are open to conversations. Day and night live coaches are available to talk about their faith or struggles. They want someone to listen and not judge them.'[3] The goal is to connect people to Christ and to a local church – but they might need to feel they belong before they are ready to believe.

 # KEY THOUGHT

He [God] has set a day when he will judge the world with justice by the man he has appointed. He has given proof of this to everyone by raising him from the dead.

---

3   http://leadnet.org/reaching-unchurched-millennials media-interruptions/

When they heard about the resurrection of the dead, some of them sneered, but others said, 'We want to hear you again on this subject...'

##  APPLICATION

What has been the starting point of conversations you have had about your faith with people who aren't Christians?

How do your non-Christian friends or family respond to the Christian story when you share it?

What stories or metaphors have you used or heard which help explain faith to non-Christians?

Think about the people you meet regularly, what are their interests; what's your point of connection?

Imagine how a conversation about faith might start with one of the people you meet regularly.

What questions might prompt people to think about faith?

Thinking about the people you've been praying for, what's the next step in reaching out to them?

## ☑ ACTION PLAN

In two teams list some of the common words and phrases we use when explaining the gospel: Sin, Repent, Lordship, Give your life to Christ etc. Swap lists and translate each of the words or phrases into everyday language that could be understood by someone with no church background. Read out and vote to give a score to each of the answers to find the winning team.

When you are next with someone and they ask you a question that relates to your faith, answer the question, then stop talking to allow them to ask you another question. People need to feel safe and in control of the conversation. Be patient and give them an answer to the question they ask. Allow them to gain understanding, step by step. Drip-feeding is more effective than drowning!

Thinking about the people on your prayer list, which simple metaphors and ideas relate to the people where you work and where you live; words and metaphors that they might understand?

 **PRAYER**

Spend time praying for each other and for the people on your prayer list, asking God for insight and wisdom as you seek to point them to Jesus.

## AIM: To cooperate with God's Holy Spirit in fulfilling Jesus' commission to us to 'Go!'

 ## GAME

Teamwork – divide into two teams and compete to carry a balloon across the room without using hands and always using two people from the team.

 ## STORY

Friendships at the school gate often become lasting, and sometimes lead to people becoming Christians. Prayer is a key factor in people finding faith for themselves. Liz and Dave got to know lots of people in their neighbourhood when their children were at the local infants' school. They had all known each other for several years when Liz and Dave decided to hold an Alpha course in their home, with the prayer backing of their church home group. They invited their friends. Liz's friend Kes was already a Christian and Dave worked with her partner Gav, so they both came. Alice and Mike were interested and came along – the meal was what interested Mike. Emma and John had a new baby. Emma stayed at home but John came; he was friends with Mike. Kate and Brian were positive; Brian was too busy, but Kate came. Together with Liz and Dave, that made a group of eight. They met each week, had a meal, watched the Alpha video and then discussed it. Sometimes Mike fell asleep, but he often asked thoughtful questions.

Ten years on Liz and Dave look back to see what fruit came from those evenings. They are still in touch with most of the people they invited to the course apart from John, who moved away when he and Emma spilt up. But Emma and Gav both became Christians. What was different about these two? Both of them had lots of people praying for them. Emma's mum was a Christian and had prayed for her all her life. Gav's wife Kes and her church had been praying for him since she became a Christian. Prayer was the single factor that made the difference.

 # SCRIPTURE

Now in the church at Antioch there were prophets and teachers: Barnabas, Simeon called Niger, Lucius of Cyrene, Manaen (who had been brought up with Herod the tetrarch) and Saul. While they were worshipping the Lord and fasting, the Holy Spirit said, 'Set apart for me Barnabas and Saul for the work to which I have called them.' So after they had fasted and prayed, they placed their hands on them and sent them off.

The two of them, sent on their way by the Holy Spirit, went down to Seleucia and sailed from there to Cyprus. When they arrived at Salamis, they proclaimed the word of God in the Jewish synagogues. John was with them as their helper.

They travelled through the whole island until they came to Paphos...

... From Paphos, Paul and his companions sailed to Perga in Pamphylia, where John left them to return to Jerusalem. From Perga they went on to Pisidian Antioch. On the Sabbath they entered the synagogue and sat down. After the reading from the Law and the Prophets, the leaders of the synagogue sent word to them, saying, 'Brothers, if you have a word of exhortation for the people, please speak.'

Standing up, Paul motioned with his hand and said: 'Fellow Israelites and you Gentiles who worship God, listen to me! The God of the people of Israel chose our ancestors ...

'... it is to us that this message of salvation has been sent. The people of Jerusalem and their rulers did not recognise Jesus, yet in condemning him they fulfilled the words of the prophets that are read every Sabbath. Though they found no proper ground for a death sentence, they asked Pilate to have him executed. When they had carried out all that was written about him, they took him down from the cross and laid him in a tomb. But God raised him from the dead, and for many days he was seen by those who had travelled with him from Galilee to Jerusalem. They are now his witnesses to our people.

'We tell you the good news: what God promised our ancestors he has fulfilled for us, their children, by raising up Jesus....

'Therefore, my friends, I want you to know that through Jesus the forgiveness of sins is proclaimed to you. Through him everyone who believes is set free from every sin, a justification you were not able to obtain under the law of Moses.'

*Acts 13: 1-39*

# ⬤ TALKING JESUS

These are the recommendations for churches from the Talking Jesus report:

1. Let's pray for the Church in our nation. We are faced with an enormous challenge but also great opportunities. Simply improving our skills or commitment will not be enough. We need God's intervention. Prayer alongside any action is essential.

2. Many people believe in Jesus' resurrection but clearly they don't recognise the impact it has on their lives. Together, let's highlight the significance of Easter and its implications for all of us.

3. We are liked. Let's recognise this and inspire confidence as a result of it, challenging the prevailing negative media image of Christians. But let's also recognise that it's not just about positive PR for Jesus followers. Let's point to Jesus himself, who calls all of us into relationship with him.

4. Let's encourage our congregations to prioritise talking about Jesus to our friends and family – one in five of them is open to him.

5. Let's prioritise reaching the Millennial generation who are open to Jesus after a Christian friend has talked to them about him.

6. Churches/denominations/networks should consider tracking our community's commitment to sharing our life and faith with those who don't know Jesus.

7. Let's discuss in our churches how we can establish as our top priority 'making Jesus known' to those who don't know him. Let's encourage the telling of stories as to how those conversations take place.

8. Let's find ways to support Christian parents in their key role of encouraging their children to become followers of Jesus.

9. Let's seriously consider the implication of the survey's findings on what influences people to become Christians and how that should impact our church life.

10. There are many people who don't know a practising Christian. How can we reach them?

# WHAT IS YOUR REFLECTION?

Acts 13 describes Paul's first missionary journey. What are the key elements in place before he starts?

How does Paul connect with his audience?

What does he tell them about Jesus?

What's your story and what's your point of connection with the five people on your prayer list?

My thoughts and notes....

 # OUR REFLECTION

Prayer was the powerhouse of the early Church. We can see that the Good News spread and lives were changed. When we ask 'Yes, but how?' we can point to their boldness; their willingness to be vulnerable; the relationships and cultural connections they made with their listeners; the strength and practicality of their love and commitment to each other… these are all important. But the key was that they prayed and God worked by his Holy Spirit to change lives. In Acts 13 they are worshipping, fasting and praying – waiting for the Holy Spirit's guidance and anointing.

The Talking Jesus report shows us that at least one in five people wants to know more about Jesus. We need to cooperate with the Holy Spirit; to be expecting God's prompting to put our faith into words and action. Let's be intentional in our prayers and our interactions with people who don't yet know Jesus.

In response to the Talking Jesus report we are encouraging Christians to commit to praying for five people – just as we have been praying through these six sessions: specific prayers for named people, expecting God to give opportunities to talk to these people about Jesus. Often it is the people we least expect to respond, who are the closest to becoming Christians. Don't dismiss people. And get together as the whole Church in your area to pray together. Expect God's presence to change your village, town or city. Invite the Holy Spirit to empower you. Prayer will be the key to transformation in your area.

When the initial Talking Jesus research was released to the 40 church leaders gathered for the Prayer Summit in Windermere in March 2015, Pastor Agu Irukwu, of the Redeemed Christian Church of God UK, responded to the initial research findings by drawing seven key lessons for our contemporary situation from the experience of the early Church. He shared with those gathered:

1.  We mustn't institutionalise what comes out of this - the early Church was a dynamic, expressive movement.

2.  The Holy Spirit must have the central role. Pastor Agu described current evangelism as: 'a lot of going but not enough waiting' and he asked 'How can we get ourselves and our churches full of the Spirit as a catalyst for evangelism in the UK?'

3.  In the early Church, prayer was the soul of the movement. The heavens belong to the highest bidder, Pastor Agu said. Our bid in prayer is way too low to birth all that we desire.

4.  There must be a demonstration of power – that is a key evangelistic tool: members of the congregation who work in the gifts of the Spirit in normal everyday situations demonstrating the power of God.

5.  The early Church walked in harmony.

The unity of the Body is critical for the evangelisation of this land. We must challenge ourselves to do more. If it is not uncomfortable, we are not doing it! If I am not open to what you bring, I short-change myself because what you bring, I don't have.

6. We preach Christ and Christ crucified. Let's not be under pressure to change the message. We do the preaching and the Holy Spirit does the convicting.

7. We need to be culturally-relevant. In the early Church, Paul was chosen not Peter. Paul was willing to engage with culture. We need strategic engagement with culture. The statistics help – knowledge is power.

 # KEY THOUGHT

'While they were worshipping the Lord and fasting, the Holy Spirit said, "Set apart for me Barnabas and Saul for the work to which I have called them." So after they had fasted and prayed, they placed their hands on them and sent them off.' Prayer and fasting were the regular practice of the early Church.

 # APPLICATION

The Redeemed Christian Church of God (RCCG) is the world's fastest growing Christian denomination. Since It began in 1952 it has grown and spread across the globe. It is no coincidence that prayer gatherings are at the heart of the movement. Twice a year 40,000 members gather for a night of prayer at London's Excel centre, praying from 8pm in the evening through until the following morning. And that's just in England. Similar prayer gatherings are held throughout the world; some bring millions of praying people together. These events build faith and put the emphasis on God's work in mission.

Is your church committed to praying for your community? How could you embed prayer into the heart of your life and the life of your church?

What priority is given to prayer in your church… and in your life? Are you learning to hear God's voice as his Holy Spirit prompts you? Revelation 22:17 says: 'The Spirit and the bride say, "Come!" And let the one who hears say, "Come!" Let the one who is thirsty come; and let the one who wishes take the free gift of the water of life.' The bride – which is the Church – is to cooperate with God's Holy Spirit in calling people to come to Jesus.

How do you know when God is prompting you to act? Share examples from your own experiences.

The RCCG churches have clear growth targets. What are the targets for growth in your church?

In the light of the Talking Jesus research how could you change the conversation among the Christians in your area from talk of decline to faith-building stories of growth?

 # ACTION PLAN

Looking back over the sessions, how has your attitude to mission changed?

What opportunities have you had to talk about Jesus with people who aren't Christians?

What about the five people on your list? How has God been answering your prayers?

Commit yourselves to pray for regularly for each other and for the people on your list, asking God for opportunities to help them discover Jesus for themselves.

# PRAYER

Pray in twos and threes for the people on your lists, asking God to bless them and to give you opportunities to serve them and talk to them about Jesus. Spend time praising God for Jesus and for all he has done for us; thank him for every response and step forward made over these six sessions.

# Leader's Guide

## TO HELP YOU LEAD

You may have led a housegroup many times before or this may be your first time. Here is some advice on how to lead these studies.

- As a group leader, you don't have to be an expert or a lecturer. You are there to facilitate the learning of the group members – helping them to discover for themselves the wisdom in God's word. You should not be doing most of the talking or dishing out the answers, whatever the group expects from you!

- You do need to be aware of the group's dynamics, however. People can be quite quick to label themselves and each other in a group situation. One person might be seen as the expert, another the moaner who always has something to complain about. One person may be labelled as quiet and not expected to contribute; another person may always jump in with something to say. Be aware of the different type of individuals in the group, but don't allow the labels to stick. You may need to encourage those who find it hard to get a word in, and quieten down those who always have something to say. Talk to members between sessions to find out how they feel about the group.

- The sessions are planned to try and engage every member in active learning. Of course you cannot force anyone to take part if they don't want to, but it won't be too easy to be a spectator. Activities that ask everyone to write down a word, or talk in twos and then report back to the group are there for a reason. They give everyone space to think and form their opinion, even if not everyone voices it out loud.

- Do adapt the sessions for your group as you feel is appropriate. Some groups may know each other very well and will be prepared to talk at a deep level. New groups may take a bit of time to get to know each other before making themselves vulnerable, but encourage members to share their lives with each other.

- You probably won't be able to tackle all the questions in each session so decide in advance which ones are most appropriate to your group and situation.

■ Encourage a number of replies to each question. The study is not about finding a single right answer, but about sharing experiences and thoughts in order to find out how to apply the Bible to people's lives.  When brainstorming, don't be too quick to evaluate the contributions. Write everything down and then have a look to see which suggestions are worth keeping.

■ Similarly, encourage everyone to ask questions, voice doubts and discuss difficulties. Some parts of the Bible are difficult to understand.  Sometimes the Christian faith throws up paradoxes. Painful things happen to us that make it difficult to see what God is doing.  A group should be a safe place to express all of this.  If discussion doesn't resolve the issue, send everyone away to pray about it between sessions, and ask your minister for advice.

■ Give yourself time in the week to read through the Bible passage and the questions.  Read the Leaders' notes for the session, as different ways of presenting the questions are sometimes suggested.  However during the session don't be too quick to come in with the answer – sometimes people need space to think.

■ Delegate as much as you like!  The easiest activities to delegate are reading the text, and the worship sessions, but there are other ways to involve the group members.  Giving people responsibility can help them own the session much more.

■ Pray for group members by name, that God would meet with them during the week.  Pray for the group session, for a constructive and helpful time.  Ask the Lord to equip you as you lead the group.

## THE STRUCTURE OF EACH SESSION

**Feedback:** find out what people remember from the previous session, or if they have been able to act during the week on what was discussed last time.

**To set the scene:** an activity or a question to get everyone thinking about the subject to be studied.

**Bible reading:** it's important actually to read the passage you are studying during the session.  Ask someone to prepare this in advance or go around the group reading a verse or two each.  Don't assume everyone will be happy to read out loud.

**Questions and activities:** adapt these as appropriate to your group. Some groups may enjoy a more activity-based approach; some may prefer just to discuss the questions. Try out some new things!

**Worship:** suggestions for creative worship and prayer are included, which give everyone an opportunity to respond to God, largely individually. Use these alongside singing or other group expressions of worship. Add a prayer time with opportunities to pray for group members and their families and friends.

**For next week:** this gives a specific task to do during the week, helping people to continue to think about or apply what they have learned.

**Further study:** suggestions are given for those people who want to study the themes further. These could be included in the hosuegroup if you feel it's appropriate and if there is time.

## WHAT YOU NEED

A list of materials that are needed is printed in each session in the Leaders' Guide. In addition you will probably need:

**Bibles:** the main Bible passage is printed in the book so that all the members can work from the same version. It is useful to have other Bibles available, or to ask everyone to bring their own, so that other passages can be referred to.

**Paper and pens:** for people who need more space than is in the book!

**Flip chart:** it is helpful to write down people's comments during a brainstorming session, so that none of the suggestions is lost. There may not be space for a proper flip chart in the average lounge, and having one may make it feel too much like a business meeting or lecture. Try getting someone to write on a big sheet of paper on the floor or coffee table, and then stick this up on the wall with blu-tack.

## GROUND RULES

How do people know what is expected of them in a group situation? Is it ever discussed, or do we just pick up clues from each other? You may find it helpful to discuss some ground rules for the group at the start of this course, even if your group has been going a long time. This also gives you an opportunity to talk about how you, as the leader, see the group. Ask everyone to think about what they want to get out of the course. How do they want the group to work? What values do they want to be part of the group's experience; honesty, respect, confidentiality?  How do they want their contributions to be treated?  You could ask everyone to write down three ground rules on slips of paper and put them in a bowl.  Pass the bowl around the group.  Each person takes out a rule and reads it, and someone collates the list.  Discuss the ground rules that have been suggested and come up with a top five.  This method enables everyone to contribute fairly anonymously.  Alternatively, if your group are all quite vocal, have a straight discussion about it!

NB Not all questions in each session are covered, some are self-explanatory.

**ICONS**

 **AIM**

 **GAME**

 **STORY**

 **SCRIPTURE**

 **TALKING JESUS**

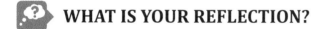 **WHAT IS YOUR REFLECTION?**

 **OUR REFLECTION**

 **KEY THOUGHT**

 **APPLICATION**

 **ACTION PLAN**

 **PRAYER**

# Session 1: Notes

## AIM: To discover what made the early Church grow

## GAME

Help people to introduce themselves by listing the types of information they might like to pass on and give them a minute or two to think of ideas. Shaking hands is an important part of this game. Before the game starts, secretly put some perfume or aftershave on your right hand. Make sure you shake hands with everyone in the room as you introduce yourselves to each other. At the end of the game, ask everyone if their right hand now smells of the perfume/ aftershave. · Conclusion: one person can have an impact spreading Good News – the 'fragrance of Jesus'.

## SCRIPTURE

Notice that Peter talked about Jesus in a way that his listeners could understand. He linked Jesus to King David. You can find the genealogy of Jesus in Matthew 1: 1-17. Here Matthew showed his Jewish audience that Jesus was descended from Abraham, the father of all Jews, and a direct descendant of David, thus fulfilling Old Testament prophecies about the Messiah.

## TALKING JESUS

For the purposes of the survey, Barna defined 'Practising Christians' as those who identify as 'Christian' but also report praying, reading the Bible and attending a church service at least monthly (and often more frequently). About one in six self-identified Christians are practising (17%), about 10% of the total adult population. The statistics used in these studies are taken from the UK Executive *Report of Perceptions of Jesus, Christians & Evangelism* which is available to download from ***www.talkingjesus.org***

# WHAT IS YOUR REFLECTION?

Encourage the group to look at Acts 1 and 2 to answer the questions in groups of two or three, before gathering together to pool your thoughts.

The Talking Jesus report refers to practising Christians as 'followers of Jesus'. When considering if friends, family and others know that you are Christians, ask yourselves if they know that being a Christian means to be a follower of Jesus, rather than simply a good citizen or something similar.

 # OUR REFLECTION

When considering how your church or other local churches differ from the early Church, avoid being negative and critical. This is not an opportunity to air gripes and grievances. And don't get side-tracked into discussing the issues that get the media's attention. Keep the focus on Jesus and the place of prayer in the early Church. The five values for a missionary church, listed in *Mission-Shaped Church* (Church House Publishing, 2004) might be a useful reference point here.

**A missionary church is focused on God the Trinity** – Worship lies at the heart of a missionary church, and to love and know God as Father, Son and Spirit is its chief inspiration and primary purpose.

**A missionary church is incarnational** – It seeks to shape itself in relation to the culture in which it is located or to which it is called.

**A missionary church is transformational** – It exists for the transformation of the community that it serves, through the power of the gospel and the Holy Spirit.

**A missionary church makes disciples** – It is active in calling people to faith in Jesus Christ. It encourages the gifting and vocation of all the people of God, and invests in the development of leaders. It is concerned for the transformation of individuals, as well as for the transformation of communities.

**A missionary church is relational** – It is characterised by welcome and hospitality. Its ethos and style are open to change when new members join.

**KEY THOUGHT**

Encourage the group to focus on God's power rather than their own weakness. Aim to build faith by noticing group members' concerns, praying about them and celebrating breakthroughs.

 **APPLICATION**

Notice the religious language and the Christian jargon that people use and make a few notes to refer back to and discuss in later sessions.

 **ACTION PLAN**

Use a stopwatch or egg timer to make sure everyone has an opportunity to speak. If there are young Christians or new Christians, invite them to speak first – they are more likely to use contemporary, everyday language rather religious clichés. Encourage people to include Jesus in their story – when did they first hear about Jesus? What was surprising about him?

 **PRAYER**

Write down the first names of people you pray for, so you can refer back to the list in the next session. Encourage the group to go on praying for the people named during the week, expecting God to provide opportunities to speak to them about Jesus.

# Session 2: Notes

 ## AIM: To refocus on THE main thing

 ## GAME

Visit *http://brainden.com/face-illusions.htm#prettyPhoto*

Print some examples of pictures that can be seen from more than one perspective, or have them lined up to show on a large screen.

 ## SCRIPTURE

If there is not time to read all of Acts 3 and 4, summarise the story so the readings are in context. Don't assume that everyone in the group knows the story.

 ## TALKING JESUS

Know your group – some group members might be fascinated by facts and figures. Others will lose interest if you spend too much time talking about the detailed statistics. Focus on the three key facts. Also, some will want to explore the more detailed evidence from Dr James Carleton-Paget and Dr Peter Williams. Encourage them to read more at home. Don't let the group get drawn away from focusing on how Peter responded to his audience and how we can respond to the people we meet today.

 ## WHAT IS YOUR REFLECTION?

Remind the group about the prayers you prayed at the end of the last session. Not everyone will have a story to tell. Let the stories of those who have talked about Jesus build the faith of the whole group, emphasising how God is responding to the corporate prayers of the group. Encourage all the group members to go on praying and looking out for opportunities to talk sensitively about Jesus.

# OUR REFLECTION

Know your group! Some people might be keen to see miracles, as they saw in Acts. Others might be terrified that God might still move in miracles. Keep the focus on Jesus and on making Jesus known in whatever ways God opens up in your context.

Reflecting on the values in Mission-Shaped Church, Paul Bayes, the current Bishop of Liverpool, wrote a comment on the 'Trinity Value' which might be helpful here: 'Christians who are equipped with the mission-shaped heart think like this: through prayer we will take the long view in God. We will be relaxed in his mission and trust the one who has won the victory: in Jesus Christ.'

 # APPLICATION AND  ACTION PLAN

No two groups are the same. Feel free to pick and choose questions and discussion points which will be most effective in helping your group to focus on Jesus and introduce others to him. Make sure that your group is a safe and encouraging place for group members to express their doubts and fears as well as celebrating successes. Remind the group that it is 'only God who makes things grow' (1 Corinthians 3:5-9).

 # PRAYER

Keep a note of the people you pray for to refer back to next week.

# Session 3: Notes

 ## AIM: Hearts and minds transformed

 ## GAME

You know your group – try this game if it is likely to be a good, fun way to start the session, helping people to relax in each other's company. Don't forget to provide lots of old newspapers and sticky tape, plus a recycling bin bag to clear away at the end and wet-wipes for newsprint-covered hands!

Alternatively show a Youtube clip from the Wacky Races and ask the rhetorical question: when are you like Muttley – pulling against what God might be doing instead of working with him? You can find a clip by searching for Youtube Wacky Races Clip or go to ***http://bit.ly/1JkfYiu***

 ## STORY

If your group won't know the cartoon characters Dick Dastardly and his side-kick Muttley from the Wacky Races, you might like to think of an alternative, negative character who works as an example for your group. Remind people that we always need to think about the most appropriate language and metaphors for the people we are talking to.

 ## SCRIPTURE

Summarise the story of Acts 10 for the group, as well as reading the specific passages. Explain how the first Christians who were converts from Judaism would have been amazed to discover that Gentiles – non-Jews – had also become Christians. Notice that Peter ensures that they have been baptised in water as well as receiving the Holy Spirit. Without getting side-tracked or picking on anyone, encourage everyone to consider baptism/ confirmation if they have not yet done so. If it arises, don't let discussion on the gift of tongues distract from the main focus of the study.

# TALKING JESUS

Focus on the key fact: When Christians talk about Jesus, one in five non-Christians say after such a conversation they felt open to an experience or encounter with Jesus. Let this fact build faith as your group prays for the people they meet.

 # WHAT IS YOUR REFLECTION?

Your group might like to revise the list of people you are praying for in the light of this discussion.

 # OUR REFLECTION

Give space to pray for each other for a fresh encounter with Jesus – but with gentleness and respect. Give opportunity for group members to ask for prayer rather than making it mandatory. Your group might prefer a written prayer which they take home to pray themselves, or they say together as a group.

Think about mission in the context of your local church and explore where limited expectations might be stifling what God's Holy Spirit might be prompting you to do.

 # APPLICATION

Help people to think about how our culture has changed. They might have become Christians many years ago when an attractional model of church worked, when people had a shorter working week, when Sundays were not sport and shopping days.

Read 1 Corinthians 3:5-9 and remember that it is God's work we are involved in.

A comment from Bishop Paul Bayes, Bishop of Liverpool, on the 'transformational value' in mission might be helpful here: 'We will look to the whole of our culture and the whole of ourselves and ask God how it can all be transformed through our community and our worship, to his glory.' [4]

---

4   *Mission-Shaped Church – Building Missionary Values* by Paul Bayes, Grove Books, 2004

## ACTION PLAN AND  PRAYER

Be specific in your prayers, naming the people you are praying for and building up each other's faith as you share how God uses you between sessions to put your faith into words and actions.

# Session 4: Notes

 **AIM: For us all to be equipped for mission in our words, deeds and values.**

 ## GAME

As well as stickers with job titles like 'nurse', 'builder', 'teacher', include some like 'witness', 'evangelist' and 'missionary'. Talk briefly at the end of the game about how everyone could have had these job titles.

 ## SCRIPTURE

Note that Lydia was likely to have been a rich and influential merchant. Purple cloth was valuable and expensive. Also, Paul did not allow cultural boundaries to stop him preaching the gospel. Women were his first converts in the area.

 ## TALKING JESUS

Adopt a 'glass half full' approach to these statistics. One in six people we talk to about Jesus wants to know more. In business terms that's a good response rate. In mission terms it gives us plenty of scope. And remember, Jesus himself did not get a 100% positive response. There are always going to be people who reject the good news. Remember '...the message of the cross is foolishness to those who are perishing, but to us who are being saved it is the power of God' (1 Corinthians 1:18).

 ## WHAT IS YOUR REFLECTION?

Encourage the group to think about the people they meet and know well – friends and family – who might be open to hearing more. Similarly, help the group to consider what spiritual hunger might look like in your community. How might your group be involved in one of the local projects that is meeting people's needs in Jesus' name?

#  OUR REFLECTION AND  APPLICATION

Encourage the group to list their hobbies and leisure interests. Are these contexts when they might meet people who don't yet follow Jesus? Could they imagine how a conversation might start naturally? If not, ask the rest of the group for their insights.

#  ACTION PLAN

When choosing an activity to run as a group, start by asking God to show you the needs of the people you are hoping to meet. Unless God indicates otherwise, start small, test what works and build on that.

A comment from Bishop Paul Bayes on the 'incarnational value' in mission might be helpful here: 'We will listen to the people living in the networks and neighbourhoods where God has put us. And we will pray and listen to what the Lord says through his word and through one another in the church and by his Spirit. And we will do that again even after we have come up with some good ideas.'[5]

#  PRAYER

If some group members find it difficult to pray aloud, ask them in advance to prepare a short written prayer to say in the prayer time.

---

5   *Mission-Shaped Church – Paul Bayes*

# Session 5: Notes

 **AIM: To share the Christian story in language and metaphors that are shaped by the hearers.**

 **GAME**

Have some fun challenging each other to use household items like a battery, a clothes brush, a watering can, a phone, kitchen scales, soap ... to talk about an aspect of the gospel. To make it more challenging you could have a buzzer to press if the 'contestant' uses Christian jargon. Use a stop watch to keep them to time.

 **STORY**

Make sure your group realises that mission has many facets – it's not only door-knocking.

 **SCRIPTURE**

Give some background from the whole chapter to show how Paul's strategy was to start at the synagogue talking to people whose background he shared, before he went to talk to Gentiles who would need to hear the gospel story from their non-Jewish perspective.

 **TALKING JESUS**

Is your group surprised by the fact that Christians are held in such high regard by non-Christians? Encourage the group to receive this information and reject more negative stereotypes.

# WHAT IS YOUR REFLECTION?

Notice that Paul doesn't make assumptions about what his listeners know. He doesn't even use Jesus' name. The response 'We want to hear you again on this subject' means his listeners are dictating the pace, and the conversation continues.

 # OUR REFLECTION

Refer back to the notes you made in Session 1. Without naming names, list the religious jargon and Christian clichés that were used when group members first told their faith stories. Encourage them to find different ways to tell their story for different listeners.

 # APPLICATION AND  ACTION PLAN

Remind people of the names on the prayer list – divide into small groups of two or three to think and pray about the language and metaphors most appropriate for each person.

If you planned a specific mission activity as part of the last session, give feedback on how plans are progressing, or how the activity went.

 # PRAYER

A comment from Bishop Paul Bayes on the 'discipling value' in mission which might be helpful here: 'We will equip ourselves as God's obedient people to be salt and light and yeast in this network culture, and we will be accountable to one another and ready to lay down our preferences for the sake of the kingdom.' [6]

---

6   *Mission-Shaped Church – Paul Bayes*

# Session 6: Notes

 **AIM: To cooperate with God's Holy Spirit in fulfilling Jesus' commission to us to 'Go!'**

 ## GAME

The aim of the game is to show that team work is vital. We are part of God's team, co-workers with him and with each other.

 ## STORY

If you have your own story to tell briefly, pass it on warts and all. Include the disappointments as well as the successes.

 ## SCRIPTURE

Prepare for the session by reading all of Acts 13 and summarise it to give the context of today's readings.

 ## TALKING JESUS

Which of these recommendations are particularly relevant for your congregation?

For the purposes of the Talking Jesus report 'Millennials' are between the ages of 18 and 35.

 ## WHAT IS YOUR REFLECTION?

Are there thoughts you'd like to pass on to your church leaders from what you have learned as a group through these sessions? Remember 'gentleness and respect' are the watchwords.

**OUR REFLECTION**

Here are some more examples of the early Church at prayer, which you might like to refer to during the session:

Acts 1:14 They all joined together constantly in prayer, along with the women and Mary the mother of Jesus, and with his brothers.

Acts 2:42 They devoted themselves to the apostles' teaching and to fellowship, to the breaking of bread and to prayer.

Acts 4:31 After they prayed, the place where they were meeting was shaken. And they were all filled with the Holy Spirit and spoke the word of God boldly.

Acts 10:9 About noon the following day as they were on their journey and approaching the city, Peter went up on the roof to pray.

Acts 12:5 So Peter was kept in prison, but the church was earnestly praying to God for him.

Acts 13:3 So after they had fasted and prayed, they placed their hands on them and sent them off.

Acts 14:23 Paul and Barnabas appointed elders for them in each church and, with prayer and fasting, committed them to the Lord, in whom they had put their trust.

Acts 16:25 About midnight Paul and Silas were praying and singing hymns to God, and the other prisoners were listening to them.

Acts 20:36 When Paul had finished speaking, he knelt down with all of them and prayed.

Acts 21:5 When it was time to leave, we left and continued on our way. All of them, including wives and children, accompanied us out of the city, and there on the beach we knelt to pray.

# APPLICATION

If you planned a specific mission activity as part of the last session, give feedback on how plans are progressing, or how the activity went.

Do refer back to your prayer list, encouraging the group to talk about how things have gone since the last session as they have looked for ways to serve others and speak about Jesus.

 # ACTION PLAN

Plan to meet again in a month or so to share how God is answering your prayers. Commit to pray for each other and for the people on your prayer lists.

 # PRAYER

A comment from Bishop Paul Bayes, which might be helpful, on the 'relational value' in mission and the commitment to proclaim the Christian faith afresh in each generation: 'We will build friendships with the people we know, and with the ones God has given us as local leaders, so that our new expression of church is "a church that feeds them with the word, a church that works with them by physically taking them by the hand, a church whose face is like that of Luke, of Mark, of John, a church that is just starting – that smells of beginnings."[1]

---

1  *Mission-Shaped Church – Paul Bayes*

# Recommended Resources for Further Study

### The Art of Connecting
### Roy Crowne and Bill Muir with Angela Little
If the very thought of evangelism gives you nightmares, this book is for you. That's because it's not even about evangelism. Well not really. It's about stories: your story, God's story and the stories of a bunch of others. Intrigued? You should be.
*Publisher: Authentic*

### The Art of Connecting Leaders' Guide
### Roy Crowne with Lorne Campbell
A leaders' guide for group work that includes two DVDs and links to the book of the same title.
*Publisher: Monarch Books*

### Sowing, Reaping, Keeping: People-sensitive Evangelism
### Laurence Singlehurst
Evangelism can seem intimidating but this book will help you tell others about Jesus by simply exploring what it means to sow the seed of faith, to reap the harvest and to nurture the faith as it grows: Sow, Reap, Keep.
*Publisher: IVP*

### Sharing Jesus: How to Put Faith Into Words
### introduced by Roy Crowne and Andy Frost
With contributions from a range of churches and ministries, Sharing Jesus looks at how to spark God conversations, ways to explain the gospel, next steps, answering tough questions and leading someone to Jesus.
*Publisher: HOPE and Share Jesus International*

### Talking Jesus: Perceptions of Jesus, Christians and Evangelism in England
Research conducted by Barna Group on behalf of the Church of England, Evangelical Alliance and HOPE. Download the executive summary and prayer resources at ***www.talkingjesus.org***. Booklets and powerpoints are also available.

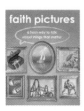

## Faith Pictures

A free, short course from Church Army designed to help Christians talk naturally to friends, neighbours and colleagues about what they believe. Find out more at **www.faithpictures.org**

## Frontline resources from the London Institute for Contemporary Christianity

Brimming with real-life stories, the combination of fresh biblical insight, humour and practical steps will not only spark your imagination; these resources will enrich your sense of wonder at the greatness and grace of the God who not only gave his life for us, but invites us to join him in his glorious, transforming work. **www.liccshop.uk**

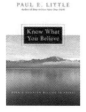

## Know What You Believe – Paul E. Little

Bestselling author Paul E. Little tackles key questions about the Christian faith and offers readers a greater appreciation of a God who has done great things to bring us into a relationship with him through Jesus Christ.
*Publisher: IVP*

## Mission-Shaped Church – Building Missionary Values
## Paul Bayes

Drawing on a wide range of reflection and resources, this booklet uses the Mission-Shaped Church report to help us shape our values before altering our structures, thus setting us free from anxiety and defensiveness and helping us be open to the missionary work of God.
*Publisher: Grove Books*

# Conversation Starters

### The Story
Luke's Gospel and Acts presented as a novel, without chapter breaks or verse numbers, for book groups and community groups to discover the journey of a lifetime.
*Publisher: Biblica & HOPE*
Find it at ***www.hopetogether.org.uk*** under the resources tab.

### The Wisdom House
DVD series written by Rob Parsons and presented by Diane Louise Jordan
Lessons for life to explore in small groups
*Publisher: Care for the Family (Based on the book published by Hodder)*
Find it at ***www.careforthefamily.org.uk/shop***

### Try Praying
A short and practical introduction to prayer for those who don't do church and are not religious. Available as a booklet and an app.
*Publisher: There is Hope*
Find it at ***www.trypraying.org*** or ***www.thereishope.co.uk***

### The Servant Queen & The King She Serves – Mark Greene and Catherine Butcher
A tribute to the Queen on her 90th birthday, which focuses on the Queen's own words to draw out the central role of her trust in Jesus Christ. The Queen talks openly about Jesus in her broadcasts to the nation. What do the people you meet think about what she says?
*Publisher: HOPE, Bible Society and LICC*
Find out more at ***www.hopetogether.org.uk***

# OTHER TITLES IN THE SPRING HARVEST BIBLE STUDIES SERIES:

## Moses
8 sessions to help find your place in God's mission and understand the issues God cares about.
SHB1366B

## Holy Spirit
6 sessions that look at what it means live a life empowered by the fullness of the Spirit.
SHB2036B

## 1 John
Get close to the Source in being, saying and doing.
SHB1839B

## Romans 8 - Inseparable
Life in Christ, in the Spirit, and in the World.
SHB1351B

## Malachi - Wholehearted
Reflections on worship, justice and the faithfulness of God.
SHB1639B

## Ephesians - United
6 sessions that reflect on the church and living a Christ-inspired lifestyle.
SHB1739B

## Daniel – Faith Under Fire
Daniel's faith was literally tested by fire, but his God – and our God – proves himself faithful in the most extreme of situations.
SHB1351B

## Passion – Finding An Unshakeable Hope
Exploring the significance of the cross and resurrection for our lives, hopes and relationships will help us grow in confidence and in the character and grace of God.
SHB1319B

## Yahweh – God In All His Fullness
7 studies which seek to guide you into a deeper grasp of the magnificence of God.
SHB1389B